YOUR KNOWLEDGE HAS VALUE

- We will publish your bachelor's and master's thesis, essays and papers

- Your own eBook and book - sold worldwide in all relevant shops

- Earn money with each sale

Upload your text at www.GRIN.com
and publish for free

Bibliographic information published by the German National Library:

The German National Library lists this publication in the National Bibliography; detailed bibliographic data are available on the Internet at http://dnb.dnb.de .

This book is copyright material and must not be copied, reproduced, transferred, distributed, leased, licensed or publicly performed or used in any way except as specifically permitted in writing by the publishers, as allowed under the terms and conditions under which it was purchased or as strictly permitted by applicable copyright law. Any unauthorized distribution or use of this text may be a direct infringement of the author s and publisher s rights and those responsible may be liable in law accordingly.

Imprint:

Copyright © 2018 GRIN Verlag
Print and binding: Books on Demand GmbH, Norderstedt Germany
ISBN: 9783668735705

This book at GRIN:

https://www.grin.com/document/429523

Mutinda Jackson

The history of the US and its influence on the world

GRIN Verlag

GRIN - Your knowledge has value

Since its foundation in 1998, GRIN has specialized in publishing academic texts by students, college teachers and other academics as e-book and printed book. The website www.grin.com is an ideal platform for presenting term papers, final papers, scientific essays, dissertations and specialist books.

Visit us on the internet:

http://www.grin.com/

http://www.facebook.com/grincom

http://www.twitter.com/grin_com

Inhaltsverzeichnis

The Social Impact of the Industrial Revolution 2

Contribution of the First Industrial Revolution to the Rise of Capitalism 3

Capitalism and the Development of Communist Theory 3

Geographic Factors to the Rise of Early Societies in Mesopotamia 3

The Process of Diffusion between Early Human Societies-Potatoes 4

Two Environmental Factors for the US Expansion 4

Martin Luther Social Changes 5

Eleanor Roosevelt Social Changes 5

The Rise of Imperialism in Africa 6

Causes, Goals and Strategies of the American Revolution 6

Causes, Goals and Strategies of the Orange Revolution in Ukraine 7

References 8

The Social Impact of the Industrial Revolution

Notably, the Industrial Revolution had diverse effects on urban and family lives, social classes and living standards. In this regard, the two principal impacts of the First Industrial Revolution include the rise of factories as well as the emergence of the Bourgeoisie. The advancement and emergence of new technologies and machinery drastically changed the division of labor, with the traditional craftsmen turning into factories to work as professionals (Desai & Potter, 2013). With the increased interest among craftsmen to work as machine operators, diverse industries cropped up, for instance the cotton textile industry, iron industry and the steam engine, facilitating the industrial factory that became the chief means of labor in the new machines. The bourgeoisie was a new group that was added by the industrial capitalism to the middle class, a class that had existed since the emergence of cities during the Middle Ages (Desai & Potter, 2013). In this sense, this term (bourgeoisie) came to include people who were involved in commerce, banking, and industry, encompassing professionals like lawyers, doctors, and even teachers as wealthy people purchased land. The lower end of the economic scale saw the shopkeepers and the craftsman.

Therefore, the aforementioned impacts are justifiable because prior to the Industrial Revolution era, most communities depended on craftsmen and farming only, before the advent of new technologies that accelerated the production of goods. As a result, people began creating interests in professional fields so as to increase their production and reduce time consuming, a phenomenon that resulted in the creation of a new class of individuals; eased by the division of labor.

Contribution of the First Industrial Revolution to the Rise of Capitalism

Scholars have affirmed that as the members of the industrial middle class were striving to reduce the barriers between the landed elites and themselves, they were also looking for ways to distance themselves from the lower (laboring) classes. Eventually, the factory workers formed an industrial proletariat although; in the first half of the 19th century they constituted a small number in the working class. Therefore, it remained evident that due to the division and change of the labor settings, the society required a bourgeoisie and a lower class for its economic development.

Capitalism and the Development of Communist Theory

Carl Marx claimed that capitalism is an unavoidable phase for the transition to communism. Marx wrote about the rise of the working class, a class that substantially existed only in capitalist societies. Moreover, it is noted that unrestricted capitalism facilitated the rise of the distinctions between the rich and the poor, differences that have evidently existed in the society over the years. Considering the Industrial Revolution and capitalism as inevitably tied together, it can be observed that communism was actually the outcome of this trend (Desai & Potter, 2013). The poor working conditions that were present in the early Industrial Revolution, and even after, can be observed to be the main aspects that made communism logical. In other words, Marx believed that this system of exploitations, where the workers were sufficiently angered by the poor living conditions, encouraged them struggle to rise against the bourgeoisie, inciting a revolution to later attain the communist utopia goal.

Geographic Factors to the Rise of Early Societies in Mesopotamia

Geography and environment have played significant roles in the development of early societies in diverse regions including Mesopotamia. Substantially, the northern Mesopotamia constitutes hills and plains, not to mention that the land is quite fertile because of the seasonal rains evident, facilitated by the rivers and streams from the mountains (Wossink, 2009). Therefore, agriculture became one of the key activities in this region, with early settlers engaging in agricultural activities for their survival. The development of agriculture expanded drastically during the Atlanticum, and this period was followed by a climate of lower temperatures. Studies demonstrate that one of the rather cold and dry spells coincided with the expansion of cities in Mesopotamia in conjunction with the foundation of the first Egyptian dynasty (Wossink, 2009).

The Process of Diffusion between Early Human Societies-Potatoes

According to historians, agriculture was practiced across the Americans from the North American eastern woodlands to the Amazon basin tropical forests. Later, the American Indians cultivated more than one-hundred crops such as squash, peppers, tomatoes, quinoa and even amaranth (Pidwirny, 2014). Some crops, especially potatoes, maize, and manioc became vital sources of food to the densely populated regions. There was a wide variety of potatoes that was cultivated in several regions of America, and observers state that these varieties remained to be the staple food in the highland South America. In other regions including Europe, diet expanded to include potatoes.

Remarkably, potato was first encountered by the Spanish conquistadors after arriving in Peru (1532) as they looked for gold, not to mention that they observed Inca miners eating *chunu*. Gradually, the Spaniards began to use potatoes as basic rations, especially after realizing that it had much significance compared to their normal activity concerning gold and silver (Pidwirny, 2014).From Spain, this crop gradually spread to Italy and other European nations in the late 1500s, and by the next century, it had entered Italy, Spain, Holland, Belgium, England, Austria, Germany, Portugal, Switzerland, Ireland and France, diffusing distinct cultures that were evident in these nations (Pidwirny, 2014). Such diffusion was justified because these were war periods that caused conflicts among communities, affecting agriculture and; hence, causing migration which has a huge correlation with cultural exchange.

Two Environmental Factors for the US Expansion

Although there are many environmental factors that played significant roles in the US development and expansion, scholars and historians have affirmed that the potato famine in Ireland in conjunction with the Dust Bowl of the 1930's were the main. The two events played a role in shaping the nation in that as the Irish potato famine devastated Ireland, it ended up invigorating Irish migration to the United States of America. As a consequence, this led to high contribution of the workforce together with the US expansion as the new immigrants moved out of the slums to find new lands of their own. Again, the 1930s drought period that was coupled with irregular rains and erosion forced farmers and landowners in the Great Plains to migrate, with the dust storms destroying any hope of land maintenance (Pidwirny, 2014). A great number of people were forced out of their land due to extreme weather, replacement of the drought-resistant prairie grass and withering of wheat. Therefore, since wheat and cotton prices fell due to overproduction, and that the drought and dust storms had substantially damaged crops, aggravating economic hardship, the farmers were justified to migrate for better living standards.

Martin Luther Social Changes

Martin Luther played a vital role during the Reformation era; a religious revolution that occurred in the sixteenth century in the Western church. Remarkably, the Reformation became the foundation of the Protestantism as it had influential political, social and economic impacts. It was a time when the church was involved in the Western Europe political life, leading to intrigues as well as political manipulations as the increasing power of the church led to bankruptcy and other social vices like corruption (Tischler, 2010). Therefore, Luther attacked the pervasion of the doctrine of the church of grace and redemption, deploring the entanglement of the free gift of grace in a complex framework of good deeds and indulgences. Here, Luther confronted the indulgence system, claiming that the pope did not have the power over purgatory and proceeded to insist that the merits of the saints' philosophy did not have the basis in the gospel. Consequently, this formed the basis for a fight towards ethical as well as theological church reform. Again, Luther's fight for ethics extended to the fight against corruption, which did not only occur in the church but also in the governmental institutions, enlightening people all over Europe and other parts of the world of the effects of this vice (Tischler, 2010).

Eleanor Roosevelt Social Changes

Eleanor Roosevelt has been noted to be an important figure in many of the most renowned social reform movements of the 20th century such as the New Deal, Women's Movement, Progressive Movement and struggle for racial justice (Johnson, 2010). Notably, Eleanor Roosevelt embraced a civil rights agenda that advocated segregation alongside championing equal opportunity. In this sense, she gave quality education her first priority among the public, which encompassed all the races, especially the African Americans. Therefore, she managed to change the education system in America as prior to her struggle; the education system was outright biased (Johnson, 2010). Again, she sufficiently fought against women discrimination in the government positions, a phenomenon that justified the election of women to the government alongside voicing out their opinions and decisions. Consequently, she managed to pressure for societal changes that resulted to cropping up of adequate respect towards the female gender.

The Rise of Imperialism in Africa

In the period between the 1870s and 1900, the African continent faced imperialist aggression from the Europeans, military invasions, diplomatic pressures as well as eventual conquest and colonization. The impetus behind the colonization of Africa encompassed three main factors: economic, social and political (Rodney, 2012). Apparently, following the abolition of the slave trade and expansion of the European capitalist alongside the Industrial Revolution, imperialism developed in the 19th century. Significantly, Europeans invaded Africa principally for economic gains; search for raw materials and markets for their finished goods, alongside settling surplus capital as evidenced by the British imperialism in East African nations such as Kenya. At the same time, the African communities put up copious forms of resistance towards the attempt of the foreigners to colonize their nations and their foreign domination, a phenomenon that saw the rise of local movements to resist European colonial policies (Rodney, 2012). The Igbo Women's War also known as the 1929 Aba Women's Revolt in southern Nigeria gives a clear example of this trend, a group that was well organized through communal associations. It was a group of women who were well organized through communal associations. Again, this group was entirely comprised of rural women who had a feeling that the impending tax imposed by the British administration, threatened their autonomy. Meanwhile, in Kenya, the Nandi community resisted the imposition of the British colonial rule over their territory, although they were defeated by the colonial masters due to the fact that they were using inferior weapons such as spears and arrows (Rodney, 2012). Satirically, the Nandi community was also defeated because some of the local communities such as the Maasai and Somalis who collaborated with the British colonialists; thus, outnumbering the Nandi community.

Causes, Goals and Strategies of the American Revolution

The American Revolutionary War of 1775-1783 that was also termed as the American War of Independence began as a war of Great Britain and former thirteen united British colonies that were under the North American sphere (Smith, 2014). Consequently, this war marked the completion phase of the political American Revolution where the imperialists had rejected the

Great Britain parliament's rights in ruling them without representation. It is vital to note that the initial goal of the British was to contain a revolutionary sentiment to Massachusetts. By the year 1975, the revolutionaries had already controlled the 13 colonial governments and formed a Continental Army. Nevertheless, petitions made to the king to intervene with the parliament on the behalf of the revolutionaries led to them being termed as traitors by the Congress, with the states proceeding with the rebellion the following year (Smith, 2014).

The response of the Americans was phenomenal as they formally declared their independence as a new nation, and in 1777, the Continentals captured an army of the British, which caused France to enter the war to side with the Americans. Notably, during this war, the British forces applied their nautical predominance to capture and occupy the coastal cities (Smith, 2014).

Causes, Goals and Strategies of the Orange Revolution in Ukraine

The Orange Revolution in the Ukraine Republic did not just present a series of protest together with mass non-violent actions in 2004-2005, but presented an event, which inspired people especially the young people (Korostelina, 2011). The main cause of this movement was the protest against massive fraud that occurred in the November 2004 presidential elections, which saw the announcement of Yanukovych who was supported by then outgoing President Kuchma. The youths remained to be a critical part of the protesters, with some of them being trained by Ukrainian dissidents who were experts on the Serbian 2000 revolution and Western pro-democratic institutions representatives (Korostelina, 2011). The volunteers were entertained with music concerts, puppet shows, provided with free foods, drinks and tents, not to mention that they were facilitated by new media technologies.

References

Desai, V. & Potter, R. (2013).*The Companion to Development Studies, 2nd Edition*. London: Routledge.

Johnson, Y. (2010). *Feminist Frontiers: Women who Shaped the Midwest*. Missouri: Truman State University Press.

Korostelina, K. (2011). *Orange Revolution in Ukraine: Inspiration of Disillusionment?* Retrieved from http://scar.gmu.edu/articles/orange-revolution-ukraine-inspiration-of-disillusionment

Pidwirny, M. (2014).*Chapter 1: Introduction to Physical Geography: Single chapter from the ebook Understanding Physical Geography*. New York: Our Planet Earth Publishing.

Rodney, W. (2012).*How Europe Underdeveloped Africa*.Nairobi: Fahamu/Pambazuka.

Smith, H. (2014). *The Second American Revolution: Closing the Four Basic Gaps of African Americans*. Bloomington: Xlibris Corporation.

Tischler, H. (2010). *Cengage Advantage Books: Introduction to Sociology*. New York: Cengage Learning.

Wossink, A. (2009). *Challenging Climate Change: Competition and Cooperation Among Pastoralists and Agriculturalists in Northern Mesopotamia (c. 3000-1600 BC)*. Leiden: Sidestone Press.

YOUR KNOWLEDGE HAS VALUE

- We will publish your bachelor's and master's thesis, essays and papers

- Your own eBook and book - sold worldwide in all relevant shops

- Earn money with each sale

Upload your text at www.GRIN.com and publish for free